When Harry Met Mummy

By Mummy Jo

An Adult Baby Story about the first few times Adult Baby Harry spent with his new Mummy

Published December 2012

Printed in the United States of America

First Printing, 2012

ISBN 978-1-291-25260-6

www.nappy.me.uk

When Harry Met Mummy

By Mummy Jo

Chapter One - How it all started

It was getting late and Harry was tired. It had been a long day, actually a long week, full of business meetings, staff appraisals and endless streams of phone calls from both contented and sometimes disgruntled clients.

Harry loved his work, the rush from a sale, the buzz of the busy office and the respect and control that he had over his colleagues gave him an air of superiority that in turn gave him an edge over others in his field. Sitting at his desk Harry's mind turned to the evening ahead, a hot bath, bottle of cider, maybe a movie... he thought to himself. All of which sounded just perfect, just what he needed.

Harry had lots of friends yet lived alone, he led a fast paced life jetting off here and there, he loved to travel, but that meant that settling down, or finding a life partner was a little trickier than he sometimes wished. He never seemed to meet quite the right person at the right time, not that Harry was really very sure who they may be, but he knew they had not yet arrived and so continued to travel, meet new people and make friends the world over.

"Harry....... Your four o clock has just arrived shall I show him in? " Harry jolted back to reality to find his PA standing at his desk with a questioning look. Shuffling his papers and opening the lid to his mac Harry smiled and said "yes".

It was about thirty minutes into the meeting, the client was chatting away and Harry was listening half heartedly whilst playing with a pile of paper clips in a pot on his desk, when he suddenly realised that he needed the toilet. Harry had not actually given himself the time to leave his desk and visit the washroom all day and now that he had suddenly felt the need he was incredibly desperate to go!

Harry crossed his legs and tried to concentrate on the meeting but it was just no use and without warning he felt a warm trickle soak the inside of his trousers. Realising what he had done Harry felt a surge of embarrassment rush over him, how ridiculous, he thought to himself... I am a grown man... When his client had finished and got up to leave Harry stayed sat at his desk, he didn't dare move, his trousers were damp and his bottom felt clammy and warm.

It was nearing six o'clock when Harry left the office, all the staff had now left for the weekend and so Harry was able to walk to his car without the damp patch on his trousers being noticed.

The fabric had almost dried now anyway but he was keen to get home and change before relaxing for the evening.

Turning the key in the door, Harry walked into his warm flat, the heating had turned on around 30 minutes earlier and the temperature was reassuringly comforting. Resting his briefcase on the dining room table, Harry kicked off his shoes and slumped into one of his huge arm chairs and within seconds was asleep.

Some time after he fell asleep there was a knock at the door, Harry woke suddenly at the sound of the letterbox banging. Had it been he wind? Harry thought starting to close his eyes again but then the doorbell rang and Harry was forced to drag himself up out of the chair and slowly made his way to the front door.

"Hi Sweety, you gonna let me in?" Harry's close friend Jane was standing on the doorstep with a huge smile. Had she said she was coming over? Harry couldn't actually remember "Of course" Harry smiled and ushered Her into the flat.

Harry liked Jane, her warm and caring nature relaxed him and they always had a laugh when ever she came by. Jane was a teacher in a local primary school, she had long mousey brown hair and huge green eyes. She was single, though always seemed to be out with one friend or another and always had the low down on who was dating or cheating on who. Harry had always had a soft spot for her and although they had never taken their relationship any further than friendship Harry felt that some how they were connected.

"Oh my!" Jane exclaimed "what on earth have you done to your trousers? " Looking down Harry realised that he was still wearing his office clothes and there was a large stain all down one leg. He had fallen asleep the moment he got in and had not had a chance to change them as he had planned.

Laughing Jane teased as she looked directly into Harry' s eyes, " it looks like you've pee'd your pants" she said with a smirk. Harry had been caught off guard, he was still feeling sleepy and didn't have a chance to think of a clever answer so he just looked at the floor in shame as the colour rushed to his cheeks.

"Wow, you really did pee your pants didn't you, what a naughty boy" Jane spoke firmly but with a mocking tone to her voice. "It seems like you need looking after more than I thought, the way your acting is more like a small child than a grown man! maybe you really are a baby" Jane continued ... "Do you need to go potty? "

A baby? A potty?! What was she talking about? Harry's mind raced. This was the second time in one day that Harry had felt silly and embarrassed and yes Babyish too... He mulled the word B. A B. Y over in his head.

"Come on" Jane was tugging at his arm and leading him into the lounge "now be a good little boy and come with Mummy" she said with a tone in her voice that both reassured and petrified him all at the same time . "We need to get you out of these soggy pee-pee clothes! ".

.............That was the very first time that Jane had babied Harry. He remembered it as if it was just yesterday. The first time she had called herself mummy and the first time they had kissed. Though not the sensual kiss that Harry had always fantasised about, No, this kiss meant so much more than sex. It was as if, in that one evening that single kiss symbolised so much, the way Jane had spoken to him, the way she had helped him undress out of his soggy trousers before running his bath and helping him to slip into the soapy bubbles, the way she had sat with him, his head in her lap as she stroked his soft curls and the way that she had looked into his eyes and told him that she needed him to be a good little boy for her ..... Harry remembered feeling so confused yet somehow he did not have the strength or the inclination to fight her and so he allowed her to take control ....

Chapter Two - The Office Encounter

It was a Tuesday afternoon, Harry had finished all of his meetings and was sitting in his office checking through the mornings orders when Jane walked in. Harry hadn't seen her for a couple of weeks as he had been out of town on business and so looked up at her with a beaming smile. " I was just passing and thought I would pop in to see how you were" Jane said with a grin. "Coffee" she gestured one hand towards the staff kitchen and removed a large packet of chocolate fingers from her bag with the other.

Harry smiled and followed Jane into the kitchen. Jane took out two mugs and spooned coffee into each then turning to face Harry she whispered "so have you missed me?"

Harry nodded, aware that his PA was in earshot and not wanting to add to the already over imaginative office gossip. Jane looked hard at him

"Would you like mummy to come over and look after you tonight honey? "
Harry Looked rather embarrassed and shuffled his feet a little, he thought about pretending that he hadn't heard what his friend had said but quickly realised that was definitely not the right thing to do.!

Why did she have to ask him this now he thought .... at work? He was sure his PA may have heard and he felt his cheeks start to blush.

Glancing up he caught his friends eye, she was giving him a questioning look and was obviously waiting for his answer. "Yes", Harry mumbled in a low voice.
"Please answer properly" Jane protested as she stirred the milk into the two coffee mugs.
Harry felt uncomfortable he knew he was cornered, the kitchen was small and she had him trapped.
"Answer me properly please" Jane repeated, but this time she had a stern look on her face – as she spoke she leant in to talk quietly in Harry's ear – "I

can see that baby has been away from Mummy for too long, I think mummy needs to show baby how important it is to answer nicely" she whispered.

Walking into his office, coffee in hand and closely followed by Jane, Harry could sense his PA's eyes follow him into the room. Jane pushed the door with her foot as she followed behind so that the door was almost shut, then she perched herself on the edge of Harry's desk and sipped her coffee.

"So??" , Jane was again starring down at Harry "Have you been a good little boy for me whilst you were away?"

Before Harry could answer Jane continued "Have you been wearing your nappy like a good baby boy or those horrid nasty big boy pants."

Harry said nothing, he was fixated on the crack in the open door and could not concentrate on a word that Jane was saying.

"Is mummy going to have to teach you a lesson for being so silly and not answering her earlier?" Jane asked sternly.

"I popped in today because i had a feeling that you were in need of my attention and i can see i was right! Mummy has come to show you just how much you need me to look after you" Jane lent in towards Harry and placing her hand on his inner thigh she squeezed hard. "You really are no more than a pathetic little baby if you can't even answer my questions" she whispered.

Harry yelped and looked up in shock "ouch" he protested "that hurt".

Jane slid her hand along Harry's leg and rested it over his crotch and gently squeezed, Harry flinched, he was only wearing boxers and Janes squeeze had sent an electric shock through his body that he felt sure would result in the inevitable hard on.

"Oh dear" Jane looked at Harry with a concerned stare "Where has your nappy gone?" she questioned.

Harry said nothing, he felt silly and small yet at the same time he could feel his cock getting hard and he knew that spelt trouble, although he reassured himself that mummy may not realise and as they were in fact in the office so there was not much she could actually do to punish him even if she did....

Jane stood up and walked over to the door, popped her head around it and spoke to Harry's PA "Can you give us ten minutes I just need to sort Harry out" Jane smiled and shut the door behind her.

Sort me out, what the hell is going on .... Harry's mind raced. This was work time, Jane knew there was a line between home life and the office so why was she doing this? He was in control in the office not her and she needed to understand that.

But Harry could not mutter even one of those thoughts, instead he just gazed up at Jane and allowed her to take control.

"Come along young man let’s get you properly dressed... what are you wearing??" Jane spoke in a disapproving tone.

Taking Harry by the hand, Jane stood him up and led him to the corner of the office, then she pulled over his swivel chair and sat down so that her face was at the same level as his trousers. Unzipping his trousers , Jane slipped her hand into Harry's Pants and as her fingers slide across his stiff cock Harry felt a surge of excitement, with her other hand she pulled her bag closer and removed a latex glove. Horrified Harry gulped, was Mummy really about to do this here!?!

Slipping the latex glove over her fingers, Jane pulled on Harry's trousers until they were resting down by his ankles and then without warning she pulled down his boxer shorts. Harry felt quite ridiculous standing virtually naked just feet from his PA and other staff, and he prayed that they would not need him for a call any time soon!

"Please bend over for mummy" Jane beckoned for Harry to bend over and then she turned him round so that he was facing the corner of he room.

"Now lets see if we can help you to remember that you are a little baby boy" Jane cooed at Harry.

Harry felt his bottom start to ache, mummy's finger was starting to gently probe at his bottom and he shuddered. Taking out a small bottle from her bag, Jane squeezed a small amount of baby oil over her latex covered finger before pushing it deep inside Harry's bottom hole.

Harry whimpered but Jane did not let up, instead she probed further. Harry was sure his Mummy had pushed something else into his bottom along with her finger, he felt it slide inside him as the latex caressed his bottom hole in every way imaginable.

Removing Her finger Jane playfully spanked Harry's bottom as she stood him up straight. "That should remind you just who you are " Jane teased.

Turning Harry to face her, Jane's attention turned to his erect cock that Harry had absolutely no way of hiding. "What on earth is going on with your silly winky?" Jane smiled.

"Come on now little boy let mummy see to that silly thing " Jane reached for the bottle of baby oil that was stood on the edge of Harry's desk. Sitting herself back down on the chair Jane eased herself closer to Harry so that her legs were wrapped around his in a locked position and then slipped her oil covered hand over his pulsating cock. With the other hand Jane reached into her pocket and produced a bright blue dummy which she pushed gently into Harry's mouth.

"Now be a good little boy for mummy and this should only take a couple of minutes" Jane spoke softly now, the stern tone to her voice had completely disappeared and Harry found himself melting into her every word.

Jane worked quickly her hand moved in a steady rhythm, her aim not to give him sexual pleasure but rather to rid

Harry of this annoying inconvenience. "Thats a good baby" Jane smiled " you make sticky for mummy like a special little baby , lets get rid of that nasty mess so that mummy can wrap you in a lovely warm nappy"'.
Harry felt his climax building and sucked hard on his dummy, mummy held his hand and squeezed gently as Harry spurted his sticky cum into her waiting hand.

Taking out a soft sweet smelling baby wipe Jane gently wiped over Harry's small babyish winky, up and over his wrinkled balls, then she pulled out a nappy from her bag and lay it out on Harry's desk, moving a pencil pot to make room for his head.

She then grabbed a cushion from the sofa in the other corner of Harry's office, lay it down and beckoned for Harry to lie on top of it on the desk, then she sprinkled a generous helping of Johnson's baby powder over his winky, gently smoothing it into all areas before wrapping Harry in a super thick nappy and a pair of thick towelling lined plastic pants.

Jane dusted off the desk and then helped Harry to put his trousers back on, his bottom was bulging from the nappy and towelling pants and Harry felt exceptionally self conscious. Jane playfully patted his bottom and smiled reassuringly at him before walking over to the office door and opening it wide enough so that both Harry's PA and a work colleague who was waiting patiently to see him could see in.
"Well I can see I have kept you far too long" Jane said with a mile as she picked up her bag.

Turning to face Harry once more, Jane commented that she would be over that evening to check on his progress and then said her goodbyes and left the office.

Harry was left sat at his desk, his bottom bulging in his thick nappy and his tummy gurgling.

Chapter Three - The Box!

It was 6.30pm when the doorbell rang, Harry remembered the time most precisely as he waddled to the door in the nappy that Mummy Jane had put him in earlier that day. Looking through the glass of the door he could see a delivery driver standing there holding a parcel.

Harry stuck just his head out of the door - his bottom was wet and his nappy was sagging and he did not want anyone to see, he felt his cheeks flush to a shade of pink but he quickly signed for the package and shut the door.

About to open the box to see what was inside, Harry stopped to read the address label, it was addressed to Jane not him! Harry was confused, Jane had never had a parcel delivered to his address before. He shook the box, eager to know what was inside, it rattled just slightly but made no noise that gave him even the slightest hint as to its contents.

Harry set the box down on the table and stared at it inquisitively, he wanted to open it but something was stopping him. Possibly he thought it was a gift for him or possibly he gulped it was a punishment. Harry pushed the box away and walked into the kitchen, just as he did he heard the front door opening and a friendly "hi sweetie" as Jane let herself in.

Walking in to the kitchen, Jane noticed the box on the table " oh good my box has arrived" Jane said with a grin. " It looks as though Mummy has come just in time" she remarked on seeing Harry's sagging nappy, " come on little one lets get you changed".

Mummy led Harry up the stairs to the nursery, this was actually Harry's spare room but it doubled up perfectly when he had no one staying and his single bed had side rails that could be attached that made him feel like he was sleeping in a little cot just like a real baby boy, which he adored. Mummy instructed Harry to stand to one side as she opened the huge walk in cupboard that housed everything

she needed. Laying a vinyl changing mat which was decorated with bright yellow ducks on the bed , Mummy beckoned for Harry to lie down.
" Oh dear you are quite stinky" mummy said creasing her nose, " let's get you out of these trousers". Lifting Harry's legs, she pulled off his trousers and removed the padded over pants that she had put him in at the office earlier that day.

Harry lay on the changing mat and allowed mummy to attend to him, he felt very icky. Mummy started by removing the tabs from his nappy and pulling back the heavy pee soaked layer to reveal Harry's very messy bottom!
" Oh dear what a stinky poo baby you are'" Mummy remarked. " It seems that mummy got here just in time, you have a horrid stinky poo poo bottom, the type that only ever belongs to a helpless little baby" Lifting Harry's legs mummy set to work wiping away all the mess that Harry had made not only around his botty hole but also all around his balls and even on his winkle. The wipes felt soft and gentle

as they glided across his skin, Harry loved the scent of the wipes it made him feel little and babyish and in turn allowed him to relax.

When mummy had finished cleaning with the wipes she lifted Harry's legs once more and slid a terry towelling nappy under him. "Mummy is putting this here under your little bottom whilst i go to get something from the bathroom"' she explained.
Mummy returned with a plastic jug of warm soapy water in one hand and a blue handled razor in the other. " Now young man" mummy said in a stern but caring voice " We cannot have nasty hairs on your bottom it just isn't right for a sweet baby boy ". Mummy worked quickly to remove every last hair then when she was done she reached for the baby powder and shook it over babies winkle as if she were powdering a donut, smiling sweetly down at Harry, mummy used the tips of her fingers to work the powder into his skin until all areas were covered. Next she took out a pot of nappy cream and started to work the cream around Harry's balls, and

babyish winkle and then down into his botty crack. Mummy pushed her cream coated fingers into Harry's botty crack and he flinched as he felt her finger probe him inside. " Keep still" mummy snapped.
"or it will hurt" Harry tried to lie as still as possible but mummies finger was poking him inside and he could not help but wiggle. mummy glared at him crossly - "Why are you being a naughty boy for your mummy" she questioned. Harry tried to explain that her fingers were poking his insides but only managed the words "' it's mummy" before a sharp slap landed on his left bottom cheek.   Harry cried and began to wriggle away from Mummy but there was nowhere for him to go. " what a naughty little boy you are" mummy exclaimed planting another slap on his bottom " are you blaming mummy for your naughtiness?" Harry didn't think that mummy wanted an answer so kept quiet. "'I know just the thing for you" mummy said with a smile that was aimed more at herself than for Harry's benefit. "Now lie here like a good boy while i pop downstairs"...

Mummy returned holding the brown box that had been delivered earlier that evening ,she set it down on he bedside table and opened the lid.

Harry lifted his head from the pillow to see what mummy was bringing out of the box, the first thing that she lifted out looked something like a long bag strap with loops. Harry looked puzzled but he didn't have to wait very long to find out what it was that mummy had in her hands.
Mummy unravelled the straps and took one of the loops and eased it over Harry's right ankle then she took the other loop and put that over his left ankle. Harry wiggled his feet playfully unaware of mummies plans.
Next mummy wrapped the straps around the bed posts and pulled on the strap until Harry's legs were wide part and his feet were locked into position, one in each side of the bed. Again Harry wiggled his feet but this time he realised that the straps had been secured tightly and so all he could do was look down at his toes in wonder.
"That should keep you from wiggling whilst mummy is seeing to you"

mummy said as she reached into the box a second time and produced another set of straps.
This time mummy attached the loops to Harry's wrists, these loops had Velcro on them and were a little softer but all the same as mummy tightened the straps around the head board Harry could feel his arms stretching and his hands become locked into position. Mummy smiled down lovingly at him, "now let's see what a good little boy you can be for mummy shall we?"

Mummy reached into the bedside drawer and pulled out a latex glove, carefully she pulled the glove over her right hand , easing her fingers in one at a time. Next she took hold of the baby oil and squirted a generous amount directly into babies bottom. "Yuk" Harry thought that feels nasty, but he just lay there and said nothing as he was not entirely sure as to what mummy had planned.
Next mummy pushed her latex covered index finger into a tub of botty cream and then in turn started to gently probe at babies botty crack, this time mummies finger slid in far more

easily, the cream on her finger allowing her to push her finger up inside baby. Harry felt mummy wiggling her finger inside him and he felt a tingle inside as she pushed her latex covered lubricated finger in and out with a slow rhythm. Harry let himself start to relax, the probing finger had been uncomfortable at first but once mummies finger was lubricated well and he had accustomed himself to the feeling of her entering him he started to calm down a little and slowly closed his eyes.

" Now little one", mummy spoke softly to Harry, "mummy is going to start you on a very special programme this evening which will allow you to be a very clever little boy for me and do poopies in your nappy without the need for horrid medicine!" Harry opened his eyes and gazed up at mummy, he so wanted to be a good little boy for her.

Mummy once more opened the box and this time she took out three black rubber things that were wider at the bottom than the top and had sort of suction cups at the base. Harry had never seen anything like them before and watched as mummy unwrapped them one by one.

Mummy explained to Harry that these were her new botty stretching toys that she would be using each time she visited so that by the end of the month Harry would be pooping his nappy without any control or choice in the matter just like the good little baby boy he should be.

Starting with the smallest, which still looked rather large to Harry, mummy dipped it into the botty cream pot and then pressed it against the opening to babies bottom.

Harry felt the rubber instrument push his bottom open, he felt as it forced his butt cheeks apart and he definitely felt as it forced its way into the depths of his rosey hole, Wow thought Harry, this feeling is really intense, Harry felt a surge of both pain and then excitement shot straight to his cock which jolted upright in anticipation. Nervously Harry looked down at it, willing it to relax but it did not, instead it throbbed and Harry wished his hands were not tied quite so tight as he had the incessant urge to wank.

Mummy continued to probe babies bottom with the rubber toy, she Massaged babies rosey hole and was pushing firm on Harry's prostate gland so that Harry could feel the pressure building up up. "Just look at your winky" mummy tutted at Harry, "that will never do! "

Mummy took an empty baby bottle from the side of the bed, harry wondered if mummy might offer him a drink of milky but instead she placed it over babies silly enlarged penis. Then she removed the rubber toy and replaced it with her finger again she continued to push hard on babies prostate gland. Reaching into the box one more time mummy pulled out a long thin black stick with a bulge on the end , then she gently eased out her finger and replaced it with the bulgy end of the weird looking stick.

Harry lay very still, his mind was racing, his cock felt like it was about to spurt and the baby bottle was starting to press into the skin as his tension mounted. Next mummy pressed a button on the bottom of the black stick and it started to vibrate. Harry's eyes started to water as Mummy pushed the vibrating tip deep inside him and it rested against babies special button in his botty.

Harry knew he couldn't take much more of this as he felt the rush of climax start to overcome him. But mummy was not about to let him be a big boy, instead she looked down at him and spoke quietly   "There's a good boy, fill the bottle up", mummy was looking down at him with a loving smile, Harry felt himself let go of all his tensions and as he looked down he realised he was cumming into the baby bottle and that his creamy cum was dribbling down the sides.
Just as the cum reach the top of the bottle and was about to drip out mummy removed the bottle from his cum soaked cock and filled the rest of it with milk before placing the teat on the top.
Mummy shook the bottle to mix babies milk with the cows milk and then placed the bottle on the side Harry looked on in dazzled bewilderment.

Surely she wouldn't make him drink that!
Mummy moved in closer to Harry, she sat really close to him, right up under his armpits so she was as close as possible. Harrys hands were still secure and they were really starting to ache now. Mummy removed a plump breast from her nursing bra, the soft skin brushed across Harrys cheek as she pushed her erect nipple firmly into babies mouth.... "Suck!" She instructed.

Harry sucked hard, he teased mummies nipple with his tongue and sucked even harder, after a minute or two baby Harry had totally relaxed and at this point Mummy removed her breast and replaced it with the baby bottle that she had placed on the side just minutes earlier. Harry clised his eyes, he was so relaxed from sucking on mummies breast that he had totally forgotten the bottles contents until he opened his eyes and looked to the bedside table where the bottle had stood, mummy saw Harry's face change with horror as it dawned on him exactly what he was drinking, but

mummy held the bottle firmly in his mouth and simply but firmly said "Suck Baby".
Harry had no choice, he was made to drink every last drop and Mummy didn't let the bottle come out of his mouth until it was ALL gone.
Once Harry had finished, mummy wiped his mouth with a terry towelling bib and then returned him to the comfort of her breast where he eventually fell fast asleep.

Chapter Four - Meeting Auntie

It was a sunday afternoon and Harry was sat at home relaxing in his sleeper suit when the phone rang, it was Jane, she was free that afternoon and was asking Harry if he would like to join her for lunch. Harry said he would love to spend the afternoon with her, it had been almost a week since he had seen her as he had been away on a business trip and he hoped that Jane would give him some of the mummy attention is so badly needed.

Jane instructed Harry to get himself dressed appropriately as she would be there in thirty minutes.

Harry opened the wardrobe, took out a pair of corded jeans and a sweater and reached for a pair of boxer shorts.

Once dressed he grabbed a pair of socks and made his way back down stairs just in time to hear the doorbell ring. Harry opened the door to find Jane and another lady waiting on the doorstep . Jane introduced her friend Jessica to Harry and explained that she would be joining them for lunch.

As they walked to the car Jane gave Harry's bottom a friendly tap, feeling no padding she gave Harry a questioning glare.
Jane decided that she would drive to the restaurant, she asked Harry to be a good boy and sit in the back so aunty Jessica could sit in the front, Harry glared at Jane, had she told her friend all about him? he felt a bit silly sat in the back seat and he wasn't sure he wanted an Aunty Jessica, after all he didn't even know her!
When they arrived Jane got out first and quickly opened the door for Harry as her car had child locks on the rear doors, as Harry got out Jane lent in to him and spoke quietly in his ear " where IS your nappy" she questioned. Harry looked at her confused, hadn't she told him to dress appropriately just an hour earlier? Maybe he had misunderstood ..

Once in the restaurant Jane chose a table in the corner that was just a few feet from a roaring open fire, Harry pulled up a chair next to Jane and to his surprise Jessica pulled up a chair

next to him so that he now sat in between the two women.
The waitress appeared to take there order, Jane read hers out first followed by Jessica but before Harry had opened his mouth to give his choices, Jane playfully squeezed his leg and spoke to the waitress " our little friend here will have a large OJ and the roast dinner please" she said smiling at the waitress who took the order down, gave Jane a comical smile and then walked away.

When the drinks arrived Jane delved into her bag and took out a blue baby beaker with a spill proof lid and straw attachment, she opened the lid and poured Harry's juice into it before handing it to him with a smile. Harry could feel the colour rushing to his cheeks, he was convinced that everybody was watching him and he felt very silly. "Come on sweety" Jessica spoke to Harry now "drink your juicy like a good little boy". She had a mocking tone to her voice and Harry did not like the way she spoke to him but mummy Jane was also looking at

him now and so he quickly took a suck on the straw to show willing.
Slowly Harry sipped the juice until it had all gone, he did his bet not to actually pick up the beaker but rather to just sip it whilst the cup was still on the table, this he felt was slightly less embarrassing. When he had finished his last sip he looked up at Jane who was chatting quietly to Jessica, " now there's a good baby boy" Jane smiled " is your juicy all gone now ?" Harry nodded. "Well I will have Aunty Jessica go get you some more then". Jane opened her purse and took our a few coins " would you mind going to the bar to get my sweet baby boy some more juices for his cup" mummy asked Jessica. Smiling, Jessica picked up the cup and headed to the bar.

When she was gone mummy turned to Harry and spoke " why are you not wearing your nappy like a good little boy" she questioned. Harry opened his mouth to explain that he must have misunderstood her request but Jane continued before he had a chance to speak. " Jessica is one of my closest

friends and therefore is your Aunty, she will help me to look after you today, I only hope you don't embarrass me but peeing in those ridiculous big boy pants you have chosen to wear! You must be a good boy and do exactly what either mummy or Aunty asks you to, do you understand?"
Harry nodded and said "yes " although he wasn't all together happy with the situation but knew that arguing with mummy Jane would only lead to trouble.

Jessica returned with the OJ just as their dinners arrived. The waitress rested the plates down on the table and handed out the cutlery. When the waitress handed Harry his cutlery Jane stopped her, we have Harry's cutlery with us she said pulling Harry's plastic fork and spoon out of her handbag. Harry didn't know where to look so he looked at the table and pretended he wasn't sat with these two women who were hell bent on making him look and feel so totally silly and babyish. Mummy Jane took out a baby wipe from her bag " show me your hands" she instructed Harry. Harry gave her his hands and mummy wiped over them one at a time " that's better" she said " now you have nice clean fingies"

Whilst mummy Jane cut up Harry's food, Aunty Jessica poured the OJ in to Harry's sipper cup then before giving it to him she opened her purse, took out two small caplet's and dropped them into the cup. Placing the lid on the beaker, Jessica now handed it to Harry, " drink up" she ordered. Harry sat at the table, he felt totally humiliated, mummy Jane had attached a napkin to his jumper that acted as a sort of bib and he was using a plastic toddler style fork and spoon to eat his roast dinner whilst sipping his OJ from his beaker. Not only this but his tummy was starting to gurgle too now, he had drunk way too much OJ and he was desperate to pee.
Realising that something was wrong, Jane turned to Harry " what's up with mummies little soldier" she said in a soft voice. " my tummy fees all wurly" Harry complained.
" Oh what a shame" teased Aunty Jessica "bet you wished you had been a good boy and worn a nappy now,

don't you?" She questioned him in a mocking tone.
Harry felt the tears beginning to swell in his eyes. “I’m not a naughty baby!” He told her.
" That was very rude young man" mummy Jane was starring at him in a disapproving way. Harry was about to complain again but he suddenly felt a strange sensation in his belly and then without warning he made a loud trumpeting noise from his bottom and he felt a warmth inside his trousers. Jessica sniggered " oh dear" she mocked "does baby need to use the potty?"
Harry did need to use the potty, but he did not move as the daunting realisation struck him that he had pooped in his big boy boxer pants!

Standing up, Jane walked over to Harry's chair and lent in to whisper in his right ear " I think we had better take you to be changed " she said.
Jane reached into her purse and pulled out what looked to Harry like an enormous key, the kind that would open the big treasure chest in the fairy

stories that mummy sometimes read him at bed time.
"I think there is a bathroom here that we can use" she said looking at Jessica now instead of Harry. " if you can take baby in I will go sort out what he needs from my car". With that Jane walked out of the restaurant, leaving Harry in the care of Aunty Jessica.

“I don’t need Punishing by you, your not my mummy!" Harry protested, There he'd said it now, he didn't like this Jessica Aunty, not one bit.
Aunty Jessica stood over Harry, her height gave her a definite advantage and she glared down at him now, daring him to move. Harry did not move but he did not smile at her either. Jessica had one hand firmly placed on Harry's chest whilst she worked quickly with her other hand, wiping around Harry's winkle and balls with the baby wipe. " you really are pathetically small" Jessica said with a tease as she finished off with the wipe. Then opening a small pot of botty cream she worked her fingers around babies nappy area until he was covered in the thick cream. " there we

go my little cherub" she smiled down at Harry but he wasn't convinced it was genuine.
Just then mummy appeared at the door, she was carrying a baby bottle containing milk " the nice waitress lady has warmed your milky up for you sweety" she spoke now to Harry who shuddered at the thought of mummy asking for this to be done, after all this was his local restaurant and he was pretty sure the waitress had recognised him when he came in.

Mummy handed Jessica a nappy, and then placed the bottle of milk on the side of the narrow change table.
"Jane, your little friend here is really such a pathetic little helpless stinky poo baby" Jessica Teased. Harry could feel himself getting grumpy when Jessica said this, her comments made him feel small and silly.
Jane giggled and pointed at Harry's pathetic looking penis, "i really do not understand why you chose not to wear a nappy today " she said. " you know full well now that now mummy uses her special botty stretching toys on your rosy hole you are unable to

control when you need to go poo poo, so this just proves that you are really no more than a helpless baby, and " she continued "with such a ridiculously small winky it really is just as well! " Jessica wrapped the nappy over babies bottom and secured it with the sticky tabs, then she stood him up and pulled his trousers back up, she could only just manage to do up the zip as the corded trousers Harry had chosen to wear were rather slim fitting and left him with a rather enormous bulging nappy area.

" Now don't you look neat " mummy cooed as he stood up waiting to be instructed what to do next. Mummy handed Jessica the bottle of milk from the side and asked her if she would like to feed baby his milky while she went to pay the bill for dinner. Harry looked at Jane with a confused and hurt expression, she always fed him, he didn't want Aunty Jessica to do it. Mummy caught a glimpse of Harry's face and gave him a reassuring pat on the bottom as she walked past. "I shouldn't be too long" she said as she left the room once more.

Jessica sat herself down on the closed toilet seat and beckoned for Harry to sit on her lap, reluctantly Harry obeyed. Jessica held the bottle to Harry's lips "come on now sweetie" she whispered "suck for Aunty" . Harry felt the soft latex teat slip between his lips and the warm comforting milk enter his mouth, he lay his head on Aunty Jessica's shoulder and as he drank she slipped her hands inside his plastic over pants and rubbed the front of his nappy.

The milk tasted good and aunties hand rubbing his nappy felt heavenly, so much so that before long Harry's nappy started to bulge at the front as his winkle pushed against the soft interior. By the time Harry had finished his milk he was wriggling and writhing in his nappy and was extremely turned on.

Jessica's took the bottle from Harry's mouth and rested it back down on the side, then she beckoned for Harry to stand up and once he had done so she walked him back over to the changing table. "Lay back down here" she commanded.

Harry lay back down on the changer, his heart was racing as Jessica started to unbutton her blouse and unclipped her bra, allowing her breast to fall just inches from Harry's face.

Aunty Jessica's boobies were much larger than Jane's and her nipples were bigger and were completely erect. Harry dared to stretch his tongue out so that the tip just touched Jessica's nipple. A bolt of excitement shot through Harry as a trickle of breast milk entered his mouth. Then he felt Jessica's nipple pushing its way through his lips. Harry started to suckle, slowly at first as he familiarised himself with the new taste. He could feel the heat of Jessica's body just inches from his and her long blonde hair brushed across his face.

Aunty Jessica was still rubbing the frontof his nappy, but as she allowed him to suckle from her heavy milk filled breast, her hand slipped inside his nappy and her fingers started to slide his foreskin up and down .

"Ooh baby has got a naughty stiffy winkle" Jessica cooed at him " what will your mummy say when she finds out you got a stiffy?" She mocked.

Harry was so caught up in the moment that he didn't answer, "well little one" Jessica continued
" we don't want mummy getting cross with you now do we?" Harry shook his head.

Aunty Jessica lifted her self up onto the change table, pushed her denim skirt up around her waist and sat astride Harry, she swooped her breasts towards Harry's face then took her right hand and squeezed her left nipple so that her breast milk squirted directly into Harry's face. Eagerly Harry poked out his tongue to lick at the creamy substance, again Jessica squired her nipple but this time she aimed straight for babies mouth, drink up your milky like a good little boy she instructed and then Aunty will be very kind and help you to get rid of that silly stiffy before mummy Jane comes back. Harry laid back, janes nipple was firmly in his mouth and he sucked hard, Jessica used her hand to loosen Harry's nappy then she slid herself over him so that his cock nudged at her moist lips, " I'm going to fuck you baby" Jessica spoke clearly in Harry's

ear. Harry continued to suck as he felt his cock enter Jessica, the taste of the breast milk and the rush that he got as she forced him to enter her resulting in an ever increasing climax.
Just as Harry felt the climax build, Jessica lifted her body from his and sat back then used her hand to pump hard on his pulsating cock. " come on little one" Jessica whispered seductively make that naughty sticky for Aunty , do it quickly mind or Aunty Jessica will not allow you to suckle her milky again," Harry felt himself release as he filled Aunty Jessica's hand with thick white cum. He felt his body relax as all his manhood disappeared and he shrunk back down to the pathetic little winkle that was there before.
Jessica cleaned Harry with a wipe before taking another nappy from the change bag that Jane had left in the room and wrapping it securely around babies bottom, then she replaced the plastic pants and zipped Harry's corded trousers back up. She stood up and straightened herself out, her hair was stuck to her face at the front so she ran her fingers through it as she replaced her shoes.

Moments later Jane returned, " I'm so sorry I was so long she apologised. I met Ben in the bar, I used to babysit for him " she explained. " Maybe he can come around one day to play" she commented smiling at baby. " I do hope you have been a good boy whilst I was away" mummy turned to Aunty Jane " I hope he didn't give you any trouble "she said winking at her friend. "No trouble at all" Jane commented " in fact he was a Very good little boy" she said as she smiled at baby. " I think I am going to very much enjoy being his Aunty".

Harry held both ladies hands as they left the restaurant . He felt totally exhausted and ready for bed. It had been a very tiring day for Harry, but he now felt relaxed and calm. after dropping Jessica at the train station jane drove bother herself and Harry back to his flat. Mummy Jane could see that Harry was tired and so led him back upstairs to the nursery and changed him out of his big boy clothes. she checked his nappy but it was still dry and so she dressed him in his soft fleece footed pyjamas, helped him

brush his teeth, picked out his favourite teddy to cuddle and tucked him snuggly up in his little baby boy bed. Jane attached the baby rails to the side of the bed so that harry could not roll out. then she sat by his side to read him his favourite bedtime story. Mummy Jane handed Harry a bottle of warm milk and kissed Harry's forehead. She stood up to leave but before she tuned out the light
she turned to Harry and spoke in a soft voice " I'm glad you have got to know Aunty Jessica today" she said kindly. " I can see that all three of us are going to have a really fun time in the future" With that mummy Jane turned out the light and bid Harry goodnight and then left her sweet little baby boy to dream his pure baby thoughts.........

Story by Mummy Jo

www.ingramcontent.com/pod-product-compliance
Ingram Content Group UK Ltd.
Pitfield, Milton Keynes, MK11 3LW, UK
UKHW020230250726
13967UKWH00001B/294

9 781291 252606